wormw

earth and honey

by Catherine Edmunds

Circaidy Gregory Press

wormwood, earth and honey

by Catherine Edmunds
published by Circaidy Gregory Press

ISBN 978-1-906451-04-2

Published by Circaidy Gregory Press
Creative Media Centre
45 Robertson St, Hastings
Sussex TN34 1HL

www.circaidygregory.co.uk

To
Sarah, Rose and Tom

About the Author

Catherine Edmunds worked for a couple of decades as a classical musician before switching careers to re-invent herself as an author and artist/illustrator. Her published stories and poems are embedded in the natural world and veer between fantasy and romance, with a dash of humour. Her artwork embraces such diverse themes as delicate portraiture and exploding beetroots. Catherine is married with three children and currently lives in North East England, between the grey North Sea and the windswept High Pennines.

Editor's Note

I first came across Catherine Edmunds' work on my own home territory – fantasy fiction. It is a genre she handles so well I assumed at first it was her speciality but I have since discovered that she is equally at home in science fiction, horror, general fiction and poetry.

The founding idea of the Circaidy Gregory Press is to give a showcase to authors who have honed their style through participation in internet or small press publications and so I am proud to say that this, her first poetry collection, clearly defines the 'Edmunds touch'. It is accessible but never trivial, warm, earthy, intelligent and – just when you begin to snuggle into the intimacy of it – spiked with fire and venom.

Kay Green November 2007

Contents

the stones of the barn

the stones of the barn
remember fear

lake wood hills
forget
but rock is old
older
oldest

man came, went
hewed rock to unnatural angles
blocks joints hard edges

a moment
soon gone
in the lake wood hills

rock doesn't see
revolving seasons
doesn't feel
the fall of the leaf

but the stones of the barn
remember fear

before man animals trees ferns
lizards and lakes

when all was fire
and the fabric
was rent
forever

Jack Frost

Jack Frost won't let go
not yet
but his strength is waning
the tenderest snowdrops
laugh in his face
it's nearly time
they say with a smile
not yet, he replies
as he nips a bud
from a foolish azalea bush

when we were ten

it's conker time, and I remember when
we hid a stash in kevin's secret den
intending to retrieve them, winners all,
but we forgot, and won't be ten again.

the flood

the palest shades of blue, as hills recede
a lake of jade, a tree, a bending reed
reflections die as skies boil grey and grim
so green must fade again as colours bleed

sea colours

five flaking rusty bolts are strongly pinned
to hold bleached wood, defeating waves and wind.
smooth rounded pebbles palest hues rescind
to darken into golden sand, chagrined.
the sea's grey-green I cannot understand,
for sky has blue enough above this land
to tint wild waters 'cross this storm-blown strand,
but sometimes sea is stronger, can withstand
such colours without care, for light it seeks.
the sea has heard me, water shifts and speaks,
allows some blue between the soaring peaks
and as I watch, the tinted water streaks,
      grey-green returns, while far away I spy
      white horses dancing, laughing at the sky.

too soon

one day nothing
the next
a host of greenfly
sucking like fury
and curling the newborn leaves
on the rose
who budded too soon

the beetle's tale

a beetle, green and shiny, told a tale
that shocked the other insects to the core
about a boy, who wanted to impale
a butterfly upon his bedroom door.
he took a net, a pin, an evil mind
and chased fritillaries across a field.
the insects listened, long legs intertwined
as beetle's tale unfolded, then revealed
the horror of the ending. wings all torn,
the butterfly limped home, and then, poor thing,
a blackbird swooped and ate it, showing scorn
for such a beauteous creature, born that spring.
     it flew with freedom only for one hour;
     and sucked sweet nectar's bliss from just one flower.

jasmine

a cave beneath a jasmine tree, full of secrets
dying leaves, wormcasts, earth and honey

branches arched above our heads, we hid
beyond the reach of people who were tall

who sniffed at jasmine, said 'too sweet'
and walked away in adult conversations

we played through summer, then the next,
and yet one more until the winter came

a chill, an aging, pruning, cutting, we grew taller
turned to teens as branches split and died

but I remember jasmine sweet, blossom buzzing
honey green when summer lived in me

fly

on the last voyage she froze
legs turned blue, angular
wings yellowed
feet stuck to poison

come spring
her desiccated body fell through twigs
a stray hair
a piece of ash

crushed underfoot by horses
giving birth to spring
she disappeared altogether

ten thousand offspring
never knew
as their fat bodies squelched through the flesh
of the dead and dying

water witch

water witch spins sand and silk
among the gentle willow warblers
hidden in the summer reeds

sand to glass and silk to cords
to strangle warblers, slice the reeds
and splice the two together

water witch swims through the mud
spears fishes tadpoles newt and frog
drinks algae fishpond slime

traps unwary fisher folk
with siren songs and silken rope
to drown in mud and sand

witchy waters shiver quietly
sleepy summer sunset sinking
fire beneath the stinking mire

remembrance

dragonfly
guide me
through dreams

grey mists lift
over channeled waters
reed bed stillness

look deep
remember the nymph
slow climbing to freedom

distant swathes of cedar
trail the water's edge
reflections bleed

fly now
to the white beach,
tall grasses
then die
dream of the time before

such gifts
ah, such gifts

5 autumn haiku

first frost.
sunflowers bow their heads –
time to go

light
creeps round corners
seeking warmth

thirty-five starlings
along the church roof
I counted them all

sunshield lowered
I squint and drive
into dying light

fallen leaves
cornflakes of childhood
crunch underfoot

the path of peril

where the wondrous withy windles
and the whiffling willow spindles
when the sylphy lady lingers
counting kittens on her fingers
if the darkling knight returns
bearing diresome deckled burns
and the siskin brindles daily
at Sir Patrick's ukulele
then we'll climb the apple tree
and defy adversity
as we walk the path of peril once again.

one, two, three, elephant

you walk into my living room
and you're fat
short and ugly and fat
short
fat
ugly
and fat

but because I'm polite
because
because
I'm nice like that
I say nothing
but I want
want
want
nothing violent
just
want

to pick you up and throw you out the window
that's all

so instead
I count

very

s l o w l y

11

berwick station

the wind fought its way round the corner
and wound up reluctantly
squeezed into my
sanctuary, my hearth, my home, my
british rail waiting room

whereupon it transmogrified into a
golden retriever

wag wag wag flap whoosh

stop being so happy you damned dog
I'm cold

somebody opened the door

the wind's companion, a small boy of
eight years or less
ran over and pounced on the dog
with much hugging and ruffling of fur

a tannoy announced the imminent arrival of
the Edinburgh express

we left the waiting room
braved the platform as the
train roared in
howling with a force ten gale that
swept us along in its wake

the dog landed first
but the little boy
twirled away in the updraft

whoosh...

haiku

blackbird tugs
as season's first worm
dies young

senryu

Eat up your cobwebs,
my antiquarian friend.
There is dust to make.

shibboleth

I'd love to abscond
with the crack in the floor but
the Tate won't allow

over the sea to annan

sixty cows grazing on skinburness marsh
tired of cumbrian grasses
looked over the water, wondering
at the land across the sea

scotland the brave
scotland the bonny
scotland the only five miles away

what do you reckon, girls?
give it a go?

and then as one
they took to the waters
they swam and they swam and they swam and they swam
across the solway firth to the land of annan

ah, the bravery
the sense of adventure
the foolhardiness of cows

five died during the crossing
and several embarrassed themselves
by becoming stranded on sinking mudflats
where kindly firefighters and coastguards
came to their rescue

farmer bowe
has farmed at silloth
for more than forty years
and is

surprised

cattle have grazed on skinburness marsh
for hundreds of years
but this has never happened before
to the best of his knowledge

he will make the trip over the border
and bring his girls back home

he thinks they were spooked by military aircraft
but I wonder
I wonder

maybe they tired of the marshes of silloth
maybe they thought
the grass looks greener and we will away
(singing) speed bonny cow
like a pig on the wing
over the sea to annan

will their milk now have a richness, a wildness
a knowledge of all that might be?
a memory of endeavour, of courage, of strength
of bovine possibility?

head in the clouds

eric was fashionably dressed
in bumptious cumulo nimbus

fleur didn't know what to do
cirrus was so last year

should she try – did she dare
wear altostratus in white?

jealousy

so jeopardy and danger flow without,
within, and round about, and where can I
escape, where fly, where run, I cry, I shout,
you rat! romance is dead. farewell. goodbye.
I slice his suits up, shave his afghan hound,
immerse his laptop in a sea of foam
with oil of lavender, because I've found
it keeps him calm (I like a happy home).
the gas is on,not lit, you understand,
a ripe banana's stuck up his exhaust,
the house is wired up wrong, you see, I planned
this out in case my desperate hand was forced.
    his chances of survival now are slim
    since lipstick on his collar told on him...

Snake

The boy wandered far too close to the river
against the advice of the elders
and there a great snake with mosaic patterning
swallowed him whole in one gulp.

He swam down its gullet and found many treasures –
a gilded crown, an ivory ankus –
he tried to turn but the way was too narrow
and so, resigned to life in the snake
he stretched himself out so the beast would not suffer
needlessly bad indigestion.

He played guessing games.
Was the snake swimming, or climbing a tree?
Slipping through grasses, sliding down burrows?
His question was answered by which creatures joined him –
a fish or an eel, a parrot or a piglet.

But then one day an ill-favoured monkey
came chattering, cackling, scratching and biting.

That was no fun, so the boy
who was thin from the darkness and squeezing
turned with great effort and swam up the gullet
until he reached the snake's fangs.

He forced its jaw wide and at last with delight
saw the green of the jungle
the stripes of a tiger
the loss of his life.

Fußball

this gadgie in germany
goes around
filling footballs with concrete

he sets them strategically
on the streets of Berlin
with a sign attached.

"can you kick it?"

arghh... broken toes broken toes broken toes

le retour

amphibious I am
fib eee yus
back again
to join the throng
at the café

don't deny
my understated grace
jet engines have been known
to blench, flinch, retrench
for lesser cause

be lenient, madame

sibling rivalry

he wanted to call the mouse sooty
because of its colour
but she, annoying as ever
named the creature
buckminsterfullerene

why? he wailed

because he's sooty
she said with a smirk

he was nonplussed
but had to accept his sister's decision
as the mouse was officially hers

the mouse had a house that was roundish
a geodesic dome, in fact
which much amused his sister
though he never knew why it should

she even gave it a tiny football
and squealed with laughter
at his confusion

he hated it when she made him feel thick
as happened so often, and always would

the mouse ran away one day so they bought another
he insisted on calling it spot
despite his sister's protestations
but mum thought it fair enough

piano

twenty years ago today
some person or persons unknown
took a piano up ben nevis
sat down, ate their sandwiches
then covered the piano with stones
because a piano is heavy
they were tired
and couldn't face carrying it
the last twenty metres or so to the summit
but
they didn't want any passing mountaineers
nicking it on the way down

they reached the top
opened a few cans of cider
celebrated
set the world to rights
then staggered back down the mountain

they forgot all about the piano

then last week,
someone found it
but couldn't play a celebratory tune
because the keyboard was missing
so they broke it up
and asked thirty passing hikers
to carry pieces down

I hope they re-assembled it
at the bottom
and found that the keyboard had magically re-appeared
and someone had an old fifty pence piece
to put in the slot
to make it play
the carpenters' greatest hits

20

then the thirty hikers
could sing along
and feel a real sense of achievement
could sing of rainy days and mondays
as clouds dropped lumps of water on them
even though it was only wednesday

bike

he sat on his motorbike
garish, resplendent,
in periwig, surcoat and pantaloons

he waited
we waited
they waited
all waited
for the fish underneath him to ripen

and when it did
the fumes exuded
took him to Tajikistan
(and back)
and then all the way to France

little piggies

little piggies on the beach
look for mum. she's out of reach.
is she streaky? is she ham?
is she gammon? even spam?

little piggies sigh and squeak.
mummy's gone, and by next week
all that's left will be some jelly
made from boiling up her belly.

top of the world

the top of the world
turned out to be
deep in a valley
(that shows all I know
of cartography)

perhaps had I turned the map
inside out
I'd have had more luck
and not had to duck
flying submarines

and if a mouse
should nibble a hole
then down we'd all go
one by one
passing the dinosaurs
primeval slime
volcanic eruptions
the beginning of time

The Hat

The fleur de lys on the carpet
gasped in astonishment
as the president stepped forward,
ski sticks in each hand,
and on his head a hat of monstrous proportions.

Above the peak which hid his eyes
arose a vast cylinder of red velvet
topped off by a small Greek cross.
The sides were decorated with strings and medals
the ribbons being made of the same fabric
as his glorious stripey trousers.

And they looked and knew
that someone should say something
because if the president entered the chamber
looking like that, then...

but of course
they were courtiers,
so the one who looked like Rasputin told him how wonderful
was his hat,
and the one with a football boot on his head said
how magnificent the trousers,
and the one wearing the exact same hat
pretended that he wasn't.

The last one offered a bottle of gin to the assembled company
whispering 'in vino veritas' to his giggling companion
but alas, gin isn't wine
and though tongues were loosened
the lies multiplied until
they all wanted one of those hats, it seemed,
so the president proposed to pass a law
that by next week they all
should have one.

And the fleur de lys on the carpet
sprang to life to raise an objection
but none would listen
so downtrodden as ever
it sank back down into its pile.

dogs might fly

a small dog flies by
paraglides through the sky
with neither rhyme nor reason
except to impress the watching knights
Sir Cei and Sir Wayne, Sir Percy, Gawain
Agravain and his twin cousin Tim

whose dysfunctional hawks
blow kisses at sparrows
to narrow the distance
betwixt and between
the medi the A and the eval

the dog doesn't care – he soars and he spins
while far down below
alone and untidy and deep in the ash grove
(down yonder green valley, where streamlets meander)
a small knotted glove curls its fingers and questions
the need for a gauntlet
when fish cannot fly and dogs can't connect
with their masters,
who've gone home to watch a thing on the telly
where some daft numpty dressed up in new armour
attempts to juggle with jelly

the dog comes home knackered
three hours later
eager to tell of his flight around the forested mountains that sank
long ago
beyond legendary Ys

nobody listens, for Wayne and his brothers
are teaching the hawks quadratic equations
and have no interest in making connections
with dogs that have learnt how to fly

mr tiklikov

I shouldn't write in this mood
when I'm liable
to answer your queries
with crunching
bones
as my teeth sink into your hand
and blood trickles
trickles
down my chin
but I'll write anyway
of small furry creatures
that make you cough
when they stick in your throat
so don't make that joke
you know the one
about the russian pharmacist
just don't
I'm not in the mood

Event Horizon

The comet flew straight and true.
Its lion head smiled and twelve fine tentacles
stretched out behind.

On the ground below
the watchers formed a pyramid
each seeking the best vantage point.

The dog who looked like a pig
climbed to the top
and squinted against the sun
not sure if he should have brought goggles.

Beneath him
were crocodiles, elephants, eland,
a brown bear who looked confused
and the ubiquitous Moomin Trolls.

A gnu called Godfrey crashed his bicycle
into the pyramid
apologised and went to find
a chilli dog with the lot.

'A what?' asked the polar bear,
quite concerned for his friend
the chihuahua,
but the others ignored his confusion.
Some hid their eyes
some cleaned their teeth
one grew a moustache
that looked very much like
Salvador Dali's appendage.

They forgot the comet
and talked instead
of heterophenomenology,
event based ontology
and the metaphysics of mind.

28

The comet was long gone
before they remembered
it wouldn't return for another
nine hundred thousand years.

They dispersed with a shrug and returned to the plains
to watch the horizon again.

The Flight of the Penguin

The penguin thought he ought to learn
to fly, but this was hard. His wings
were short and stumpy. Then a friend
(called Bob) came floating by and said:

"I have a plan! Let's try this out."
"Try what?" asked Peter, as a tern
flew overhead as if to scoff,
and left a poo on Peter's head.

"I hate that bird! Oh, how I yearn
to drop a plop into his nest!"
Bob eyed his friend with some concern,
"Here, let me help you to ascend."

He lit the fuse and felt the burn,
as Peter flew to Penguin's End.

The Ballad of Shane and Mavis

Erik came first – a snail as tall as a ten foot door,
he slimed his way forward
leaving behind a trail of gloop
for Trevor and Alan to follow.

Sheriff Shane was quick on the draw,
but how do you fight such a monstrous sight?
Deputy Mavis pursed her lips
and whistled in C sharp minor.

The snails slowed down imperceptibly
and came to a halt twelve yards or so
in front of Shane and Mavis

The Sheriff was at a loss.
He put his gun back into its holster
and wished himself back in Alabama
while Mavis changed to B flat major
and gazed at her lover's nose.

It's all very well, being first on the draw,
but the snails were unarmed.
Shane refused to fire the first shot,
knowing it must be the last.

Erik laughed with the sound of thistles;
waggled antennae and smirked at Mavis,
then slimed his way forward closely followed
by Trevor and Alan, slowly at first,
but a burst of unaccountable speed
took Mavis and Shane by surprise.

The unfortunate lawman knew at last
that he should have fired first,
for later that night, he and Mavis
were supper for three hungry snails.

fearless

she arrived in a gale
and sailed into port

(or the beachside caff, to be strictly accurate;
opened last year by a windswept dignitary
who admired the paddling pool
which much to my surprise is still clean)

(unlike the dignitary.
but I digress.)

the coastguard was called
to open double doors
allowing her entry

her weight? I don't know
but her ancient companion
on his trike
was a coracle to her liner

her tonnage astounded
wrapped in a tent of navy nylon
escorted by a pilot carer

we shifted to one side
as she hove into view
tables and chairs were swiftly removed
her progress assured

she refuelled with tea and eccles cakes
before braving the wind and the rain
and scattering skate-boarders in her wake
she rode forth once again

fearless

killing time

I'm killing time and writing rhyme
while waiting for the paint to dry.
I murdered him, and for my crime
I'm killing time and writing rhyme
disguising bloodstains, gore and slime.
Thick paint will hide my guilt. That's why
I'm killing time and writing rhyme
while waiting for the paint to dry.

grandfather's beard

grandfather's beard
bifurcates
halfway down his chest

one half goes this way
and one half doesn't
but gets tangled with his pocket watch
and knotted into the chain

he says a word I'm not
supposed to know
as he tries to read his watch
untwisting strands
that threaten to de-regulate
his careful life

I often ask him
the time

tangerine dreams

tangerine dreams
of sunlit skies
cerulean blue
mediterranean climes

the dream fades
he waits in a basket
tries to evade
destiny
as motes of danger
flecks of despair
settle on his
mottled pocked skin

then one day
a pungency says
I shouldn't have waited
should've consumed
sooner

blue green grey…
mould go away, go away…

too late

thrown in the bin
squashed beneath
an empty tin
and some bacon rinds

I buy more
but what fate
is in store
for these?

blue ghosts

Caspar
Balthasar
Melchior

translucent ghosts
still wandering
after a star they'll never find again
resigned to their fate on a piece of card
a fragment
a cheapening
a loss

once they were wise men
who could fool a king
and protect a child

but now?
a picture hung too long in the sun
loses itself
until only blue ghosts remain

Caspar
Melchior
Balthasar

resonant names
of misty memory
fading
fading away

the diver

he sought the stream that took him beneath
but waves caught him
turned him into a slippery thing
that slid between water white water

ship's on the horizon too far too far
slip through water churning foaming slipslipslip
sink deep sink down become fish become eel sea thing
swim laugh swim breathe swimswimswim

City of Adelaide

Slipway slip sliding
from birth on the Wear
to last berth in Irvine.

Tall ship, fast clipper
forgotten and rotting
farewell, my sweet City of Adelaide.

Running Stitch

The mending pile beckons.
Fallen hems are no problem
as creases are sharp
and a stitch in time…

Returning the needle
to its faded felt home
memories awaken.

1967 – top in needlework;
a pinnacle, no question,
embroidering a needle case
in Miss Charman's class
little thinking
so many years later
I'd notice
a slip.

One stitch is too long,
upsetting the rhythm
of brown grey yarn
on green… green…
Memory fails.
I cannot recall what you call
that fabric with all
the small holes
at all.

But what if…

What if I'd sewn with
utter precision,
omitting the error
that flawed the perfection?

Could I have come higher than first?

the burning of ice

the winter-bound tip of a twig held in ice
until the release of a distant thaw
is like that old trick where your finger is gripped
by a cold woven tube, and you pull to escape
but it holds you despite your cries for release
(I'd forgotten the burning of ice)

I try to snap off the tip of the twig, but I can't –
I twist and I spiral the sinews that cut, cut and tear
bleeding rivers of cranberries
pips and bits that get stuck in my teeth
though I floss with sinews that slice through my gums
like ribbons of couch grass
remember, remember; never tear couch grass
don't hold it too tight between finger and thumb,
don't blow it too hard, lest it scream
and the white bull will charge, but the fence is too weak
I did it – he skidded on ice and he fell

the fall of the bull wasn't funny at all, no more
than the twisting of ice in the bucket
with pilchards that cut my arms, black red and raw.
Remember: don't burn, don't freeze, don't scream
eat pilchards, ride bulls, twist sinews, light twigs
find that immolation redeems, so burn,
burn like ice, and the years that erupted have gone,
turned to ash that settles and melts into spring

Beloved City

Justine shivers and pulls her coat closer.
The gendarme's been talking to maman for ages,
so Justine scowls and purses her lips –
an expression that twenty years from now
will drive her adorable Pierre to the arms
of an artist named Jean-Henri.

The wind makes her ears feel like someone has punched them.
At three years old, she must wear a thin bonnet
that ties beneath her chin with a string
that cuts and chafes as she stands on the bench,
her be-ribboned doll by her side.

She stamps her feet as she waits for maman,
whose thoughts are far away, for she's seen
down the bank, a couple embrace in the autumn,
and maman remembers a time, a glass of wine,
a red hat, a sash, a poster of Piaf that floated
away past the leafless trees into winter.

The gendarme stops talking as no one is listening.
He would shrug, except that
his great coat prevents such a movement
so he turns, sees the lovers and smiles.
The moment is broken
by Justine, who squints and reminds him to
pick the artichoke out of his teeth.

The couple move on beneath brown paper skies.
Maman picks up Justine, who wails, for
Cécile (the doll) has dropped off the bench
and the gendarme would help
but his coat is too tight to bend over
or so he says, though the truth is this child
has poisoned his will to live.

He shakes his head and wanders away,
thinks of his wife and the slime and the grease
that floated on last night's bouillabaisse,
remembers the heartburn and wonders again;
how can she cook so terribly
in this, his beloved city?

the persistence of prunes

two prunes
sold for twice
their expected value
at spinks
the auctioneers
yesterday

they had been used
by the resistance
to smuggle maps
behind enemy lines

I had to read the article
several times
and am still not quite sure
how the prunes
managed their daring feat

but I enjoyed the story

too much war stuff
is offensive glorification
of the unutterably unspeakable

not enough
about the simple heroism
of fruit

so let us remember
the persistence of prunes
in times of danger
the honour of oranges
the pacifism of peaches
who never go to war

sixty years on
the persistent prunes
still survive

a peach would have passed away
long ago
dropping its stone
to start a new life

but I'd sooner be a peach
than a prune

lycoperdon giganteum

deep in the darkness
of hidden deception
in underground places
you grow

spreading fibrous tendrils
through rich loamy soil
testing, gently
sourcing nourishment
wheedling your way
and awaiting your time.

through winter's cool death
and spring's proud decision
sweet summer's abundance.

not yet, not yet.

autumn arrives;
and the time of fruition
the thrust through to freedom.

a white nodule
grows overnight,
and then, when first light
hits the new day's dawning
you swell, pregnant, obscene
bulbous, desiring explosion
to scatter your spores
your millions of children

and yet...

fecund destiny's denied
for I have found you
and sliced you
and diced you
and fried you
in olive oil
with garlic
sea salt
pepper
a good dash of Beaujolais...

alas, poor puffball.
consumed.

excision

black ink blots drop
onto my drawing
it's lost
can't be fixed
save with razor
sharp craft knife
but then – do I dare?
where life drains
away in the pain of
excising the blot,
not a chance
this'll work.
out, damned spot

Iguana

There's an iguana on the wall behind me
oiled onto canvas and stuck behind glass.
If I turn round I'll be caught by his eyes
so I tap tap away on my computer keyboard
ignoring cold stinking breath on my neck.
Paintings can't hurt me. They really can't. Can they?
The touch of his tongue flicking in and out, in and out,
tells me I might be mistaken.

cernunnos

beltane is nigh
light fires, catch spring, seek earth's dark womb
breed wildlings

hunter and hunted
lead your ride
thunder hoof fall

seed and outnumber the stars, cernunnos
turn your seven tined head to the sun
then hunt, run again, capture and kill

your dark face is sweet at the very end
and your unhewn mystery revealed

Pete's Pipe

after the gig we repair to the Greyhound
and Pete lights his pipe.

not many pipes around these days
but the smell makes me smile.

when I was little, Dad smoked a pipe
which was kept on a rack in the dining room

where I'd sit and play on the lino floor
with fingernails full of plasticine

winding up my tin motorbike
and watching it go round and round and round

building a village from plywood cut-outs
with schools and houses and a zebra crossing
and all the while, there in the background
the pervasive smell of Dad's pipe.

which all got too much for Mum one day
so the pipe was banished to the garden shed.

now as I chat to Pete in the Greyhound
downing our pints of Black Sheep bitter

he laughs, 'that's why I smoke it,' he says.
'all the girls love a pipe.'

unto death

the third constant wife retired unto death
her mouthless starvation where once she ate
bog myrtle ripe bilberry heather

short hope, long gone, she'd craved escape
rejecting jollity redundant in derry
without any doubt her doorway out
let her out let her swim out
of this earth pushing down on eyeballs the grit
the anguish denying bright strangulation where once
her fable told lies simultaneously without fear or fret
where once
once
the farmer from derry
caught her in blue absolution

too late
regardless of worth replenishing her with silver
coins on eyelids won't keep out dirt ingrained in his fingers
his touch
his touch
remember slick scales yellow eye
swim further upstream swim swim swim

now underground waiting for the ferryman fisherman
she tries to lift the rock swim through earth

too late

in derry he farms for the third fourth fifth sixth generation
laughs now she's followed the others
pours his poison fillets his fish and laughs again unto death

secret windings

behind the door
the door in the corner
lie balls of wool
wound tightly around
one another, tied
with knots and false twistings

how did this come to resemble my brain?
I'd tell you,
but first I must
untangle my thoughts
once so clear, now bound
with nylon that sparkles with static
whenever I think
so that shimmering pain
cuts across
my escape

one day
one day I'm going to
open the door
the door in the corner
and slice through the nylon
using my knife
you know the one?
the one you say I must put away?
the one you say I mustn't use
for slicing and dicing my flesh?

one day
one day I think I'll tangle
and strangle your thoughts
using miles and miles of the secret windings
I'll find in your bowels
tie you tight
slice and dice, slice and dice, slice and dice

48

the dig

she kneels in the trench
trowel in hand
scrapes away a layer of dirt
happy to work on in the midday sun
while everyone else has gone for a pint
or is sucking a strawberry mivvi

they mustn't find out
not now
not ever

many hundreds of years ago
she dropped it somewhere hereabouts
returned too late
and he caught her and killed her but yet
the babies were safe
so long as nobody found it

she held on tight to a fading existence
slept on chalk beneath nine barrow down
waited until the time was right
to return to langton matravers

she kneels in the trench
scrapes the dirt
lets the sun dry out faint markings
mixes up soil
(post hole? what post hole?)
pockets a slither of bone

soon discovered and sacked for her troubles
at least the job is done

close at hand

and so to bed, she said
without telling of dark mares
or calling fruition on nightly malingering
walking in grass so malicious
and munchingly stewed with fresh beans and honey

but why?
she can't know she won't know she can't tell never tell nor will tell
will not tell

it's passing capricious, reliant, you know
is it really? in truth?
no, crash out, it's no good
as kestrels sigh warnings she cannot hear, will not hear
reaching, delicious one single match
standingly dangled obtusively juicily
candles drip blood in this light

tonight, Madagascar, she teases,
tomorrow? get drunk
we'll wander with sorrel
and so?
fade away, don't stay with burnt toast
so she said and she smiled and all of the while
he wondered, and tried to remember.

for words given lightly when moons drift apart
are not worth the paper they laid on the rocks
beneath Brooke's dell, decisive, or not
where languishing muscles forlornly redundant
await final decomposition

but February came and she promised
not here, not now, but westbound past Paddington.
Brooke? ah no, that's another tale
told to frighten the pine forest's subtlety.
stay close, she said, once again, as a warning
sleep now. forget. the circle is broken
and railway lines flow to the sea.

flight

he's flown there again over six thousand miles
to bathe in dark spices and find his mind
and fade fast away despite all we could say

the result for those who won't follow his lead
is an argument over mount board
glue sticks and what time should we begin?

where boundaries are blurred
no problem is found, but four dimensions
separate fast. three plus one need each other

remember snot? coloured stuff for kids?
you pull a big blob with small hands
and it stretches and stretches and stretches and

pfft. pulled into two separate pieces. if he doesn't
look after himself better than this, if he finds
one day he can't return, then pfft. gone.

split. his stolid parents wonder what happened
to their sylph-like son and the rest of us
sit still, sharpen pencils, smooth down paper.

black hole

she drove
like a maniac
at the lamp post
on the central reservation
wrapped her car around it
at such high speed
that the vehicle
spaghettified
as it ran round
and round
and round
and round
never ending
sucking her in
as she'd always hoped
it would one day

channel hopping

sky news at
I don't know that you even noticed
football, less football, less football, less
as my legs, aching, aching, aching,
bloody silent radio 3 again
no, can't do this
realised their timetable was wrong, bbc radio 4 news
tea, maybe tea, tea usually helps, please? make me a cup of tea?
at rose cottage in pankot.
ah, good
I'm sorry, I didn't mean to disturb you
birdsong still, didn't notice before
an extraordinary experience
not so late after all
their behaviour was fantastic, a glimpse really of what this culture
can be
music playing, bodies swaying... no, I didn't write that
and does this day put that disappointing day six days ago
supporting the rolling stones? who cares. who bloody cares
but the next year going on to win the championship
can't stand that band, never could, misogynist arseholes
you will forgive me for saying this
birdsong, windsong, remember, remember, remember,
I thought we should have won
I remember when, I was ten and you
a man who's ending his career at celtic with great dignity
they like the music, why do they like the music? it's not birdsong
sometimes the english arrogance doesn't always accept how big they
are
it's nothing
the passion!
irrelevant
quite immense –

without meaning
speaks volumes, volumes,
while you have meaning
while five live brings you one sporting event
more meaning than I can bear
obviously everyone says it's better than it was
please play that song, please
I remember paris in '49
thank you
before that we heard the beat and errrm…
fantastic
absolutely fantastic

release

he sat in the corner and shivered
causing another finger to fall

only three left now

not bad, not bad, he thought
five hundred years of desiccation
were bound to leave their mark

this summer, he'd hoped for release

but it had rained
incessantly
relentlessly

tiresomely

today, the sun shone at last
the final threads of the antique drapes gave up their substance to the
light
and fell

the beam sought his face as he smiled
and crumbled
to dust

shadow

he feared his shadow

I knew
by the way he held himself
with arms bent
and staring eyes

how could this elongated
dark mass
emanate from his feet?

his eyes were round
pin prick pupils staring
sideways

he feared his shadow

I wondered
why

curtains

bricks
red and black
grime on the floor
two bottles
empty

a chair
red
tubular steel
white curtains knotted
around its legs
looking

like a body
a bunch of brown flowers
on its lap
withered

five yards away
another
crumpled
on the floor
too far away to help

light fading
night soon

too late
to draw

curtains

crescent moon

he wanders at night by a crescent moon
hunting for hedgehogs
for once, long ago
he committed a heinous crime

he took two dozen prickly beasts
to a place where they were not welcome

they ate and destroyed
not the insects and bugs he was hoping they'd find
but the eggs of a golden plover.

in autumn
the moon turns from silver to gold
reminding him of his crime

so he wanders the streets by a crescent moon
and breaks through the privet surrounding the gardens
where sometimes he finds
a hedgehog
sipping a slug
or crunching a beetle to death

he takes the beast
slits open its belly
looking for eggs

he knows...

he knows he must pay for his terrible crime
returning the eggs
to the plover

folded paper flies

attend to your own daffodils
the business of growth will corrode
not extend
your silky florets.
each granule awaits the hydraulic impulse.

a drop of tincture
thyme, hyssop, sweet cicely
a mass of scratching twigs hung over rafters
bound tight and precious

scrape my skin raw
help me forget this squadron of flies
that launch a torpedo across my universe

culpepper
please
distil this essence
stop cicadas from stealing my mind

but hold –
the colour is low.
water flows like origami and is rotten.

mary

yesterday
she walked between trees
from chapel to ruin.

followed a path of sorrel
where the ground dips
into a muddy trap

raced past garden walls
neat bricks, secret delights
peaches,
stolen on a whim

remembered, too late
that sorrel poisons
the unwary

into the distance

1

they face away from me into the distance
but what do i care
they're dead
if they ever existed at all

maybe he just imagined them
maybe he thinks that's how couples should be
maybe he was never in a couple
that's why I can't see
their faces

2

she wears a dark shawl over her head
and rests her hand on his shoulder
oblivious, he stands in his long cloak
wearing a hat like a mushroom

tree roots rise from the ground like prehensile limbs
reaching towards the couple
the bold slash of the trunk veers into one corner
branches sweep the other way
leaving a bright gap

now I see what they see
the moon
(may I mention the moon in a poem?
I must.
you wanted the picture)

grey pines angle up to the right
where a darker tree droops anguish
which tells us?
who knows

3

I walk into through the frame and
into the distance
I can do this because i am poet
creator too in my way

I turn to face the couple
wondering what i will see
what they will say if we speak

with my back to the moonlight
my shadow is cast on their faces
so I move to one side
and there
oh
there
no
I didn't
shouldn't

they have no faces
he didn't paint them
of course not
how could he?

call yourself poet? creator?
you couldn't create them
could you
I tell myself as I leave

impasse

he looked to the left
hair blowing like twigs in the wind
eyes wide open behind goggles

she faced to the right
her beak tied tight with an elastic band
to keep her quiet

he had done this

it hurt, oh it hurt
her eyes swivelled in their sockets
and looked this way and that
but never in the same direction

between them
lost and lonely
an egg
ticking away
quietly

South of the Border

South of the border lies a land
where locusts fly over white sand.
With never a care
I'll meet my love there
with my bare
ringless hand.

South of the border we'll embrace
where the sun baked rocks leave no trace
of the lies we told
in the grey north cold
of pure gold
in that place.

South of the border, free at last
no need for wealth – that's in the past.
The gemstones we find
are all in the mind.
(Limbs entwined,
hold me fast.)

South of the border there are fires
that burn out these heady desires
as we turn to dust
no more love or trust
just our lust
on twin pyres.

South of the border I will die
dreaming of northlands, asking why
I left that grey land
no ring on my hand
for white sand
and a lie.

so in love

the bruises
well he did them
yes
he hit me
but you see
it was because
because

he wanted me
and he couldn't

and so he hit
and then he could
and yes
i know that's wrong
but

he loves me you see
and he wanted

so it's ok
really

it's not a police matter
they're just bruises
they'll heal

just a domestic
you know?

we're so in love

so he hits me now and again
that's ok, really, it's ok
don't worry, there there, it'll be ok
don't worry don't worry don't worry
don't cry
he can't stand crying
so best not to cry

it's not a police matter

we're so in love
you see

deception

white whiskers twitching
she stared into the headlights of his eyes
and lied

no, you've got it all wrong
she said
making sure not to blink
making sure to angle her body to hide
what mustn't be seen

he decided to believe her
after all
why not?

why shouldn't she sit there shivering in a blanket
and trousers three sizes too big?

she held her breath
then smiled him permission to leave

five minutes later she judged it safe
to weep

white noise

echoes of the big bang, he said
all frequencies
that's what you're hearing

all frequencies mask
additions, I said

what do you mean?

the screams, I said
screams?
the pain

each time you pluck a rose
I scratch myself, he laughed
is that what you mean?

no, I said

I mean
the scream of the rose

damaged

he draws the back of his hand
across his eyes
and sniffs
not crying
no, he's not crying
just a touch of hay fever

eyes clearer now
fingers walk over the car's flank
past careful sandings and many repairs

there's a scratch – a new one – six inches, perhaps?
he examines it in microscopic detail
marvelling at multi-coloured layers of paint

(eyes sting again. paint allergy? must be)

he concentrates on the hot trickle
that creeps down his face

it helps him forget his mother's dry curses
calling on dead men to disembowel her children
it helps him forget
the smell on her breath on her clothes in her hair
the sticky wet cut on his temple
shaped like the edge of a bottle
of bombay sapphire gin

a fly senses blood and corruption
waltzes in zig-zags and seeks out his face
he lashes out
all the fury of seventeen years in one blow

a small dent is added to the car's wing
and the fly departs
unharmed

a rasping sound
his foot's kicked a twelve inch monkey wrench
he picks it up, nods once to the car
then goes to look for his mother

Tom doesn't see

fording the river was always a problem
the horses don't mind
cool water flows by

one horse snorts
shakes his head
there are flies exploring his eyelashes

Peter is puzzled
why this stillness?
he wags his tail
waits
wags it again
but Tom doesn't see the puppy
jump this way and that

a cloud passes over while Tom thinks of Ruthie
sweet Ruthie
and Ruthie's dad Joe
and last May on the green

when Simeon Tanner asked her to dance
and took her away and wed her and beat her
but it could have been...

Ruthie's dad knew best

Tom sits on the haywain stuck in the river
while Willie Lott's dog
jumps
and wags his tail

but Tom doesn't see

death in the garden

limpet leaf spreads
across your mouth breath stops
foxgloves three inches more this morning
clover mauve end of flowers
end of life
seed serrated teasel leaf

sharp, wasn't it

embrowned leaves
the taste of your eyes
feather fledgling house sparrow flies by follows family
how many survive
maybe one or two

heat sun dirt dust burning
birds flapping moss
dead brown cuckoospit bug grows
needs water
failing red stems mint fire leaves burn
dry flamed wallflowers

do you burn?
worm wriggling paving hot sun
wriggles slow dies

fern fronds green now hide brown
beneath red spider mites crawling
kill them
fly lands kill stamp don't allow ugliness
only death in the garden

I saw your garden
so die amongst your roses you never
you never scratched me with roses
so die

counting slowly

drive through rain clenched teeth
grind to a halt
wait
one minute
over the solway firth it's a view
but you can't photograph it
one minute, two
the sun's always
always

wrong

wait be patient
three, five, eight hours
fly overhead in monstrous improbability

I don't care any more

the girl at the desk is new
can't work the system
gets it wrong
again and again and again

eight, thirteen, twenty-one

looks up
with a closed face
call that a key? rubbish
piece of plastic flimsy magnetic strip
rubbish

no matter
I take it and walk the dead corridor
too late
thirty-four hours
stifled by carpet

it's a spot of turbulence
no more

bet you don't even remember
broken promises in the back of a van
crumpled
I had to laugh

rain go away
fly swift strong higher higher
don't come back
fifty-five, eighty-nine
you'll never know
will you

I still wait
holding my broken rendezvous
counting slowly

Truth and Lies

I lied to you, and now you'll guess the truth.
How long, I wonder? Minutes? No. too late.
He's watching, daring me to lift my eyes
and answer silent questions. Must I? Now?
He nods. I turn to you, and yes, I know,
you won't believe a single word I say.

The way we kissed – ye gods – what can I say?
My breath, my lips, my tongue told you the truth
but how will you believe me, now you know
that I'm not who I said. The hour is late
yet you insist on having answers now.
I see it, read it, in your narrowed eyes.

Remember when we met, and those same eyes
were full of words I longed to hear you say?
Desire is gone. You're full of anger now
as bit by bit you learn the sordid truth.
There's one who would defend me, but she's late
I doubt she'll come now. Doubt you'll ever know.

He's telling you the 'facts'. What does he know?
He cannot guess. He didn't see our eyes.
That meeting. I was there – I wasn't late
but he was there before me. He will say
that what he saw and heard is all the truth,
but things have changed, it isn't like that now.

I lied, but that was then and this is now
and though he thinks I love him, he can't know
the way you touched me, showed me my own truth,
taught me to see and cleared my clouded eyes,
but what's the point of telling him? He'll say
he's got the proof. My words will come too late.

What proof? Why, papers. Sad but true. It's late
to show you these. But here. Look at them now.
You see? I had to do it, orders say
I must seduce you, find out all you know
and yet... you never saw my lies. Your eyes
failed utterly to comprehend the truth.

So here we are. The truth has come too late.
Within your eyes lies death. No pity now.
You'll never know what else I longed to say...

to the distant beloved

there was a storm last night
and a rainbow
I felt you there
your arm around my waist
radiance arching
such distances
light curving around
connecting us
my golden boy
smiling
at the end of the arc
as clouds gather
walk with me in colours

the animus of the inanimate

he sits, not two feet away
the repository of my memories
small enough to nestle in my hand
innocent enough to fool the unwary

I download my sorrow through touch

he sits and watches
silent forever
his story untold

first there was boudin, courbet, whistler
then turner, seascapes and skies
from trouville to tentsmuir
in snowstorms in sunlight on sundays high days holidays
prussian raw sienna monestial phthalo alizarin
cadmium pale, no payne's grey today

I remember he had
a big head
no, not vain, I mean literally big
all those brains

he finally grew into that head, that hair, that beard
the way some kids grow at last into their feet

there's a tear in my eye
from chopping up chillis
I forgot
to wash
my hands

and still he sits and watches and waits
though I distract myself
with paintings and wine
and poetry

Tintoretto Smiles

Jacopo Tintoretto smiles at me
through paper, blue and faded, barely there,
with charcoal marks, exquisite artistry
that moves, inspires me, drives me to despair.
But why? you ask. I'll tell you. Hear my tale
of sick desire, a tally of dark need
for his sweet face. He senses that I'll fail
to find his shadow now. I can't succeed –
he left four centuries and more ago,
and yet... he smiles with solemn antique eyes
that pierce my soul. I'll take some chalk. I know
we'll never meet, my sketch is full of lies,
    my skill is lacking, lines go all awry,
    yet I will draw my true love ere I die.

polperro

a seagull calls, and I remember waves,
a tiny shrimp, deep rock pools, secret caves,
a bed of sand, your hand upon my thigh –
a feeling this is not how one behaves...

Between the Trees

Between the trees there lives a leafy sprite
whose green disguise conceals a scaly hide.
At night, the woodland creatures fear the sight
of this fell creature seeking out his bride.
Beyond the trees there lives a maiden fair
who danced with dragons as a tiny child.
Now grown, she must remember to beware
this greenish imp who'll make their fire seem mild.
Or so they told her, yet when these two meet,
the dragon child and green snake in the wood,
the maid will wonder why she feared his heat
and learn how he has been misunderstood.
        Beneath the trees they love and laugh and kiss
        the maiden giggling at her lover's hissssss...

the wind

on a high cliff
my lover's hands run through my hair.
the north wind
tears at my consciousness
insisting I remember
intimacy

mittens

thirty years later
he kissed her
she wondered why it had taken so long

for weeks after that she indulged herself
in cheery erotica
fearful of waiting another three decades
before he went further
by which time she'd be, what, oh lord, far too old

the answer – a tardis?
flying through wormholes?
a slingshot around the sun?

travel back, try again, don't be so uptight
so fearful so cold walking hand in hand
past the pitch and putt all those years ago

cold? it was frosty. remember?
of course she was cold
she wanted to put her hand in her pocket
instead of feeling it turn to ice
which his frigid fingers quite failed to thaw
clasp and caress as they might

okay, a thought: make sure to pack mittens
when travelling back through space and time

so romantic, mittens

she smiled and decided perhaps thirty years
on from now wasn't really so long
though the physics was scary, but still...

she snuggled down, went back to sleep pleased to find
that her mind was improving with age

the barque

she sailed into the cove
turquoise water
salt taste of sea spray
scent of childhood

sun beat down in waves
warming pink thrift on the cliff top
the cry of the gulls
ah, the cry of the gulls

I saw her
pointed
squinted against the sun
then she was gone
and they laughed at me
nobody else saw her
nobody else remembered how to see

Richmond Castle

I chased his squealing laughter
up stairs hidden in whistling walls
he shrieked with delight then
fled and ran away with the wind

I lingered too long
rain clouded my sight
and I lost him
though I ran back through the great hall's echoes
he'd vanished

a chuckle mocked me
I turned
chased back up the staircase
breathless with anger

imp, stop taunting me

I reached the last of the battlements
the top of a turret
he stuck out his tongue and jumped

I wanted to follow him
to fly with the storm and laugh

the castle still whistled its mournful tune
I descended slowly with wind wrapped around me
cushioning me comforting me telling me to wait

summer's end

season's departed
gone woodlice slugs ants
the butterfly you caught ate laughed

forked tongue indigo eyes

burnt out by summer heat light
red spider mite white marble
pepper-pot bright apples dripping
stamped hard forged now

take on camouflage rust ochre
and wonder what if

munching chicory wild mallow poison
digging up green potatoes daffodil bulbs

what if

cherry tree falling

what if you moved on to another garden
and I followed

slip hiss slither away away away
catch me if you can
larkspur juniper heather
in another garden
tomorrow

Fiction by Catherine Edmunds

The Sand in the Painting

An Impressionist seascape fascinates student Emma on a visit to an art gallery. Grains of sand are caught forever in the painting – trapped – just as she is in her claustrophobic relationship with antiques dealer John. The next two weeks will decide their future, as Emma is increasingly drawn towards the enigmatic Toby. Only Evan knows Toby's secret, and how it will fundamentally affect any relationship with Emma. He is torn between patient confidentiality and his duty to his friend, complicated by his own frustrated desires. An unexpected stay at a seaside cottage brings matters to a head. Meanwhile, John's life is slowly falling apart. The outrageous Renée can sense the impending crisis, but knows from past experience how hard it is to help John. Each one of them must learn to face their individual failings and deal with them – to come to terms with their own sand in the painting.

"Catherine Edmunds has a natural talent for designing believable characters, strong settings and a powerful mastery of the complexities and inner workings of the 'human condition'. " - Louis P Burns, Upstate Renegade Productions.

'The Sand in the Painting' ISBN 1-4241-1168 is available from Amazon and all major online bookstores. For further details, and to read extracts from the novel, please visit Catherine's website

http://www.freewebs.com/catherineedmunds/

High Fantasy from Catherine Edmunds

I Have A Daughter

"I have a daughter."

My father's deep tones rang out, commanding silence, and the moment I'd been dreading since I turned sixteen finally arrived. I clutched Shull's fur and watched intently from behind the grill that had helped keep me invisible all these years.

The tall warrior's eyes lit up. These were the first words of a ritual, and barbarian or no, he knew them well, but had never expected to hear them himself. None in the hall would have know of my existence; the fact that my father had a daughter. There was a murmuring of surprise, then a hushing to silence.

"I have a daughter," my father repeated, softly this time, and this time the warrior responded. The ritualistic words were spoken harshly, his voice cracking with the strain of sudden unexpected hope.

"I have need of a wife..."

Catherine's short story, "I Have a Daughter" appears in the High Fantasy anthology: **The Sleepless Sands**, ISBN 978-0-9553429-3-6, published by Earlyworks Press, available from independent bookshops or direct from the publisher online.

More poetry from Catherine Edmunds

Catherine's work appears in the Earlyworks Press anthologies

Digitally Organic

and

Shoogle Tide

www.earlyworkspress.co.uk